Impact
on Earth

The Impact of
BUILDINGS
AND CITIES

Tim Cooke

Crabtree Publishing Company
www.crabtreebooks.com

CRABTREE
PUBLISHING COMPANY
WWW.CRABTREEBOOKS.COM

Author: Tim Cooke

Editorial director: Kathy Middleton

Editor: Ellen Rodger

Picture Manager: Sophie Mortimer

Design Manager: Keith Davis

Children's Publisher: Anne O'Daly

Production coordinator and prepress: Ken Wright

Print coordinator: Katherine Berti

Photo credits
(t=top, b= bottom, l=left, r=right, c=center)

Front Cover: Shutterstock / bodom, r; All other images from Shutterstock

Interior: Alamy: NASA Image Collection 8; Dreamstime: Steve Allen 12; Getty Images: Blom UK 21, Niels Christian Vilmann 25; iStock: tomlamela 5; Shutterstock: Rich Carey 15, B. Claude 11, f11photo 27, Nady Ginzburg 19, David Hughes 14, Liona Ignalova 7, Ali Jawwad 20, Lopolo 13, Stuart Monk 23, R Nagy 22, Trong Nguyyen 9, Pierluigi Palazzi 24, Patrick Foto 26, Peera_stockfoto 4, Ppictures 6, Dan Schreiber 10, Suarav027 17, Takamex 18, testing 16, AndjeiV V 28, vasabii 29.

Library and Archives Canada Cataloguing in Publication

Title: The impact of buildings and cities / Tim Cooke.
Names: Cooke, Tim, 1961- author.
Description: Series statement: Impact on Earth | Includes index.
Identifiers: Canadiana (print) 20200165836 |
  Canadiana (ebook) 20200165844 |
  ISBN 9780778774341 (hardcover) |
  ISBN 9780778774402 (softcover) |
  ISBN 9781427125132 (HTML)
Subjects: LCSH: Urban ecology (Sociology)—Juvenile literature.
  | LCSH: Sustainable urban development—Juvenile literature.
  | LCSH: City planning—Juvenile literature. | LCSH: Human
  settlements—Environmental aspects—Juvenile literature. |
  LCSH: Urban pollution—Juvenile literature.
Classification: LCC HT241 .C66 2020 | DDC j307.1/416—dc23

Library of Congress Cataloging-in-Publication Data

CIP available at the Library of Congress

LCCN: 2019058747

Printed in the U.S.A./022020/CG20200102

Published in Canada
Crabtree Publishing
616 Welland Avenue
St. Catharines, ON
L2M 5V6

Published in the United States
Crabtree Publishing
PMB 59051
350 Fifth Ave, 59th Floor
New York, NY 10118

Contents

What Are Cities?

By 2050, nearly two-thirds of the world's population will live in cities. This will have a huge impact on Earth.

A city is a large settlement, with many homes, workplaces, stores, and other services. Even small cities have a **population** of more than 10,000 people. Large cities might have millions of inhabitants. Cities are often spread out over wide areas. New York City, for example, covers nearly 470 square miles (1,213 sq km).

Cities, such as Tokyo, are large centers of human activity. Altogether, the world's cities produce about 70 percent of the greenhouse gases **released** into the air. The gases trap the Sun's heat, so Earth gets warmer.

People Power!

About half the world's population live in cities. Together, that many people can have a major impact. If city dwellers used less power or ate less meat, for example, that would cut down on the amount of carbon released into the **atmosphere**. These changes could improve life for everyone on the planet.

55% Percentage of Earth's population living in cities
82% Percentage of the world's city dwellers living in USA

Problems for People

Cities create many problems. Housing is often expensive. The poorest inhabitants live in poor-quality homes. Traffic jams cause air **pollution**. Cities need a huge amount of energy to run, and create a lot of waste. Cities impact the natural world. Growing cities disturb wildlife and their habitats. They also interrupt necessary natural events, such as floods.

Crowded Cities

The center of a city is a high-density area. This means many people usually live close to one another in buildings packed together. Large buildings often have many small apartments, where people have only a little room. They may not have any outdoor space. There is more noise from neighbors. In the **suburbs** which surround a city, there is more room. Buildings are farther apart. Houses might have yards.

This crowded housing is in Athens, Greece. In high-density areas like this, a large number of people live in a small area.

Building Up

Many cities have little unused space at ground level. People build upward instead. Modern apartment and office buildings often have more than 40 stories, or floors. The core, or center, of buildings must hold up floors made of iron beams and glass. It is usually made of strong material such as concrete. The Burj Khalifa in Dubai is the world's tallest structure. The glass is coated with material that reflects the Sun's heat. The building gets less hot and needs less energy to cool it down.

163 Number of floors in the Burj Khalifa
2,716 feet (828 m) Height of the Burj Khalifa

Using Energy

Cities use a lot of energy. They have miles of street lights. There are offices and homes full of people who use energy. Families might cook food at the same time or watch TV. In winter, people turn on the lights and heating. In summer, they use air conditioning. Older buildings are often badly **insulated**. They release heat into the outside air. This makes the buildings inefficient at using energy.

Why Worry?

Cities have an impact both on their surroundings and on the lives of their residents.

Homes, malls, streets, and highways cover most of the land in a city. There is not a lot of green space other than yards or parks. Birds and raccoons adapt to living in cities. Animals such as mice and rats become pests. Around the city edges are garbage dumps and industrial sites. They can pollute streams and fields.

These images taken from space show how the city of Santiago, Chile, grew between 1985 (top) and 2010 (bottom). The city (blue) spread over countryside (red).

Urban Sprawl

As cities grow, suburbs spread around the edges. This is known as urban sprawl. Suburbs are built on wild land or farmland. People in suburbs often drive into the city to work. This creates more traffic and more pollution. Montreal, Canada, and Brisbane, Australia, are two cities with large areas of urban sprawl.

76% **Percentage of the population of Brisbane, Australia, who live in separate houses, rather than apartment buildings or townhouses**

Stretched Services

Cities grow bigger as more people arrive to look for work. A higher demand for places to live means homes can become very expensive. More people also means the need for more schools and medical care. Law enforcement services are stretched, which can lead to high levels of crime. As a city grows, these problems can get worse.

Cities and the Environment

As cities spread, they have a growing impact on their **environment**. They replace natural habitats, such as forests or grasslands. Large numbers of trees are often cut down to make room for construction. This not only impacts wildlife, it also affects humans. Trees help remove harmful **carbon dioxide** from the air through their leaves. Reducing the number of trees worsens the quality of the air in cities.

The flat land along rivers that overflow their banks regularly is called a foodplain. When rivers flood in a natural landscape, the water gradually sinks into the soft ground.

Feeding Animals

Wild birds and animals cannot always find food in cities. You can help by planting flowers in your yard or in a windowbox. Flowers attract bees and other insects. The insects are food for larger animals, such as shrews or lizards. Some people like to hang outdoor bird feeders. Not all cities encourage this, as it attracts other wildlife, too.

1.9 million Population in danger from coastal flooding in Kolkata, India

$1 trillion Annual cost of possible flood damage to coastal cities around the world

Trapping the Water

Many cities are located near rivers. When these rivers flood, water spills onto the low-lying land beside them. In a natural environment, the water drains away into the soft ground. In a city, much of the ground is covered in concrete. There is nowhere for the water to sink in. This can cause serious flooding in the city.

Problems with Buildings

Buildings have a range of environmental impacts. They also directly affect the lives of the people who use them.

Construction uses materials such as wood, glass, and stone. The way these materials are made can harm the environment. A tree cut for lumber can take many years to replace. Buildings need a lot of energy to heat and light them. They use lots of water for drinking, bathing, and for washing machines.

In cities such as Valparaiso, Chile, homes are often made from thin wood, tin, or board. They release heat into the atmosphere.

Turn Down the Thermostat

Small changes can reduce how much energy you use at home. Sometimes, we have heating on even if it is not very cold. You could ask your parents to turn down the heating at home by one or two degrees. If you feel cold, put on a sweater! It is a small change—but if we all did it, it would make a big difference.

35% Percentage of heat lost through the walls of a house that isn't insulated

25% Percentage of heat lost through the roof

Inefficient Homes

Many buildings use more energy than they need. In poorly built homes, windows and doors often fit badly, letting heat escape outside. That means it requires more energy to heat the building, as well as cool it by air conditioning. Poor quality homes can also damage people's health. Mold can grow if a home is damp, causing breathing problems.

Harming the Environment

Stone is dug out of the ground in areas of land called quarries. This damages the landscape and natural habitats in which plants and animals live. Materials dug out of quarries, such as the soft stone used to make cement, are not **sustainable**. There is only a limited supply that can be easily dug out of the ground and it cannot be replaced. Clearing trees so land can be used for another purpose also does damage. When trees are cut down, their roots stop holding the soil together. Without tree roots, the soil on hillsides is in danger of being washed away by rain.

Huge machines dig stone and other materials out of the ground at a quarry. Explosives are sometimes used to blast rock loose from the walls. These practices create large open pits.

Using Different Materials

One way to reduce harm is to reuse materials. Bricks, glass, and wood can be reused from old buildings. Another solution is to use sustainable materials. Straw is made from dried plant stalks. It is cheap and easy to grow. Straw bales can be used to build walls. Covered with dried mud or plaster, they help keep out wind and rain and keep in heat. This new idea is based on ancient methods of building.

1.5 miles (2.5 km)

Length of Thornton Quarry, Illinois, one of the largest sources of stone used for construction in the United States

TECHNOLOGY SOLUTIONS

Sustainable Materials

Newer, more sustainable materials are now being used in construction, including a form of wood made from old newspapers. Mashed with water, the paper is dried in hard sheets. Some builders are also using bark from trees as siding to cover the walls of houses. Bark can be removed without damaging a tree.

Cities and Pollution

Cities are large contributors to one of the planet's biggest problems. Motor vehicles, factories, and homes add to air pollution.

In many large cities, you can actually see the air pollution in the form of smog. A mixing of pollution and fog, smog is made of billions of particles of soot from fires used for heating or cooking or from factories or power plants that burn **fuel**. It also comes from vehicle **exhaust**.

In some cities such as Beijing, China, people wear masks over their mouths when they go outdoors. The masks prevent them from breathing in soot from smog.

Delhi

Delhi, the capital of India, is one of the worst-polluted cities in the world. Dirty air has damaged the lungs of half the children there. One of the main causes of pollution is road traffic. Other sources include wood fires, industrial pollution, dust from construction sites, and exhaust from electrical generators that burn diesel fuel.

2.2 million Number of children in Delhi whose lungs are damaged by breathing polluted air

1/30th Size of soot particles in smog compared to thickness of a human hair

Other Forms of Pollution

Cities cause other kinds of pollution. Large numbers of people create a lot of trash. Some trash is **recycled**, but some is thrown away in huge dumps called landfills. Landfills give off greenhouse gases that add to the warming of Earth. Dumps also pollute the local land and water.

Traffic Congestion

Most vehicles run on gasoline or diesel. These are **fossil fuels** that are drilled from the ground. The fuels are burned in engines to produce energy. This burning produces exhaust that is released through the tail pipe. Exhaust contains waste gases, called greenhouse gases, that collect in the atmosphere. The gases prevent the Sun's heat from reflecting off Earth back into space. This heats Earth's atmosphere and contributes to **climate change**.

These cars are stuck in a traffic jam in Bangkok, Thailand. A car sitting in traffic releases more exhaust than a moving car.

Smart Cities

Cities are using different ways to try to cut the amount of exhaust cars emit. Smart traffic signals detect when cars are waiting. Computers change red and green lights to try to keep traffic moving. Some cities charge a fee to take cars into downtown areas. Charging a higher fee to vehicles with high emissions reduces the amount of cars in the area.

45–55 mph (70-88 km/h)
Speed at which car engines burn fuel most efficiently

7.5 mph (12 km/h)
Average speed of traffic in Beijing, China

Noise and Light Pollution

Transportation, construction, and other activities also cause noise pollution. This can damage people's hearing or cause stress that harms their health. Light from streetlights, buildings, and car headlights can result in a city that is never in darkness. This light pollution can disturb people's sleep and upset wildlife. It can also prevent city dwellers from seeing the stars at night.

What's Being Done?

It is possible to change buildings and cities so they are less damaging to Earth. In some cases, however, changes can be hard to make.

Cities are busy places with many residents. We can't just pull them down and start again. Some cities were first built hundreds or thousands of years ago. It can be hard to change old buildings to reduce their impact on the environment.

One of the oldest planned cities was Mohenjo Daro in modern-day Pakistan. Built around 2500 BCE, its streets were laid out in a grid pattern.

Superblocks

In Barcelona, Spain, the city council created superblocks. The aim was to reduce noise and pollution from cars. A superblock is a group of nine blocks. The space in the center is a public space for pedestrians and cyclists. The only vehicles allowed are delivery vehicles and those belonging to residents.

6 mph (10 km/h)

Speed limit in a superblock, not much faster than walking speed

Changing the Face of Cities

Cities facing challenges to change can still be improved. Buildings can be made better at using energy. Old windows can be replaced by modern glass that holds in heat. New elevated, or raised, highways can take cars away from residential areas. This reduces air pollution and noise.

Recovering Old Land

As cities grow, some parts become run down or abandoned for use. City planners try to bring these sites back into use. This is called regeneration. Many cities around the world have run-down areas. They include places where factories once operated. They might be districts such as docks or freight yards that have closed down. These areas are often near the city center, close to jobs and stores and restaurants. Once regnerated, they have become popular places to work and live.

When the docks in an area of London, England, closed decades ago, the land and remaining buildings became run down. Today it has new office buildings and luxury homes.

The High Line

Except for its famous Central Park, Manhattan in New York City has little green space. Work began in 2006 on an old railroad line that ran through Manhattan on elevated tracks. The old line was turned into a 1.45-mile (2.33-km) long park, with paths and gardens. The High Line is very popular with residents and tourists.

5 million Number of yearly visitors to the High Line

1.5 billion Number of passengers on the Paris metro, or subway, each year

Public Transportation

One way to reduce problems such as pollution is by getting people out of their cars. New city districts can have rail or subway networks, streetcars, or bus services. These public systems carry large numbers of people and use less fuel than cars. Wide sidewalks and bicycle paths encourage people to walk or bike to work.

Future Developments

In the future, it is estimated that even more of the world's population will live in cities. Cities will grow even bigger to house them.

New cities can be planned from scratch. Buildings can be designed to be energy efficient. The city can use renewable energy sources. Planners can include green spaces in their plans. There can be good public transportation links so people don't need to use cars.

Buildings can add plants in living walls and roof gardens. These features allow residents to grow their own food. Plants also remove carbon dioxide from the atmosphere.

From Waste to Energy

Copenhagen in Denmark is one of the world's greenest cities. The Amager Bakke power station is by the waterfront in the city. It turns waste into energy for **electricity** and heat. It also serves as a place for people to enjoy. At the top is a park with hiking trails and a climbing wall. There is also an artificial ski and snowboarding slope that is open year round.

150,000 Homes powered by Amager Bakke each year

300 Truckloads of waste that arrive at the plant each day

An Eco Town

New cities can use up-to-date green technology. Elmsbrook in central England is a **zero carbon** town. That means the town does not release carbon into the atmosphere. All the houses have **solar panels** and extra layers of glass in the windows to hold in heat. The bathrooms use rainwater. There are bike paths, walkways, bus stops, and charging stations for electric cars.

In 2018, Shanghai in China was home to more than 24 million people. By 2050, that number is expected to rise to more than 50 million people.

Megacities

Some experts believe that future cities will continue to spread in area. Some will join up to form huge "megacities." Megacities are cities with more than 10 million inhabitants. There are already megacities around the world. Most are in Asia. Tokyo, Japan, is the megacity with the largest population. More than 38 million people live there. The megacities in North America are New York City and Los Angeles. Other megacities include Mexico City in Mexico, Cairo in Egypt, and Jakarta in Indonesia.

Cities of Regions

Megacities are collections of many local neighborhoods. Residents often feel more attached to their particular area, rather than to the whole city. As megacities expand, neighborhoods can be linked together by mass transit systems. New construction between neighborhoods can be planned to be eco-friendly. This will allow more people to live in cities and limit their impact on the environment.

47 Number of megacities in the world in 2020

1950 Year the population of New York City reached 10 million

TECHNOLOGY SOLUTIONS

Tokyo Megacity

Japan's capital, Tokyo, is the largest city in the world. It was badly damaged by an earthquake in 1923 and by bombing in World War II (1939–1945). Each time, the Japanese rebuilt the city. They planned new suburbs with high-density housing. The suburbs were planned with transportation links to make moving around as easy as possible.

Your Turn!

Currently, about two-thirds of the electricity produced in the world is created by burning fossil fuels such as oil. We can all reduce our impact on the planet by reducing how much energy we use in our homes.

Gather the Evidence

Start by taking a survey in your home. Record the information in a list for each room.

- How many outside doors and windows are there?
- What are the major appliances, such as TV, refrigerator, or dishwasher?
- How many lightbulbs are there?

How many lightbulbs are there in each room? How about other devices that use electricity?

> **Low-energy lightbulbs use about a third as much energy as traditional lightbulbs.**

Ask Questions

Use your list to figure out answers to the following questions.

- Could appliances be used less frequently?
- Are lights left on in empty rooms?
- Do the windows and doors have gaps around them that let warm or cold air out of the house?

Reduce Your Usage

Where can you see ways to save energy? Encourage your family to turn off lights when they leave a room. Replace old lightbulbs with new, low-energy lightbulbs. Turn off electrical devices and chargers when they are not in use. Devices left on standby still use electricity. Seal leaky windows and doors with tape. Encourage your family to use less water by taking quick showers rather than baths. All these small changes can have a large effect!

Glossary

atmosphere The layers of gases that surround Earth

carbon dioxide A gas in the atmosphere, released when living things exhale and by burning fossil fuels

climate change The gradual warming of Earth as a result of human activity

electricity A flow of tiny charged particles that can power devices such as lights and computers

environment The natural world around us

exhaust Waste gases given off when fuel is burned

fossil fuels Fuels that formed from the remains of living things that died millions of years ago

fuel A substance that is burned to produce heat or power

greenhouse gases Gases such as carbon dioxide that build up in the atmosphere and trap heat

insulated Treated in a way that preserves heat

pollution The adding of harmful substances into an environment

population The people who live in a particular place

recycled Used again, either in its original form or in a new form

solar panels Devices that use sunlight to generate electricity

suburbs Residential areas on the edges of a town or city

sustainable Able to be maintained, such as a source of power that will never run out

zero carbon Does not give out any carbon

Find Out More

Books

Amson-Bradshaw, Georgia. *The Houses We Build (Eco Steam)*. Cavendish Square, 2019.

Greenan, Amy. *Constructing Towns and Cities (Impacting Earth: How People Change the Land)*. PowerKids Press, 2018.

Howell, Izzi. *Population and Settlement (Geofacts)*. Crabtree Publishing, 2018.

Websites

Find out what a home energy auditor does by visiting the NASA Climate Kids website.
climatekids.nasa.gov/career-auditor/

Visit the Royal Geography Society website, with facts and information about megacities.
www.rgs.org/schools/teaching-resources/discovering-megacities/

This website looks at the factors that go into designing and building an eco-friendly home.
www.homebuilding.co.uk/what-is-an-eco-home/

Index